Words from my heart

Eleri Wynne

Copyright © 2015 Eleri Wynne
All rights reserved.

ISBN-13: 978-1517218157
ISBN-10: 1517218152

PREFACE

This collection of poems was written over a period of ten months. I had no thought or intention of writing poetry, but the first lines of the first poem came into my heart during one dark night when I was aware of spiritual opposition. At more or less the same time a song of triumph rose up within me, and by the next day a poem had emerged. Following this first poem, I found myself in different situations where I wanted to encourage friends and found it easier to express what was in my heart through a poem rather than to do so in a conversation. Then came a number of instances where I myself was in need of spiritual direction. I sought the Lord, read His word, tried to express what I felt was going on and looked for direction from Him. The end result was this present collection of poems.

I am not attempting to attain any high literary standard, but rather expressing thoughts and words from my heart, and this is how I would like them to be understood.

Eleri Wynne

22nd July 2015

Table of Contents

FEAR NOT THE NIGHT 4

SAY NOT 5

HIS LIGHT 6

FEAR NOT THE POISONED DART 7

DO NOT STRUGGLE SO..9

YOUR STRENGTH SHALL COME… 11

I SEND THE SNOW..13

STARS 14

THE YOUNGER SON...16

THE QUESTION I WOULD ASK...21

MY LIFE IN YOU 23

HIS PEACE 25

LIFE ETERNAL...28

THE TRUTH 30

HIS WAYS..33

SIN 34

LORD AND KING 36

WORSHIP 41

JEW AND GENTILE 42

MY SHEEP HEAR MY VOICE 48

BE STILL	51
WEAKNESS	53
WHAT I WOULD SAY	56
PRIDE	59
HARDSHIP	61
BEING MISUNDERSTOOD	63
WHERE JOY IS FOUND	65
SERVING HIM	67
JUDGING OTHERS	70
THERE IS A LIFE. . .	72
NEW LIFE	74
THE SUFFERINGS OF CHRIST	77
THERE IS A HOLY FIRE	79
THANKSGIVING	81
HOLY GROUND	83
YOU HAVE A WAY	84
KNOWING HIM	86
PASSING JUDGMENT	88
THAT WHICH COMES OUT OF THE HEART	90
HIS SUPPLY	92
THE KINGDOM OF GOD	94
I KNOW NOT HOW	97

FEAR NOT THE NIGHT

Fear not
The night,
Within your heart
There burns
A stronger, brighter light.
He is the One
Who guides you
Through the darkest, fiercest night.
Fear not its terror,
Nor its darkest hour.
Trust Him
Who also is
The morning star.

And He then finally
Shall dissipate the night
And all its darkness.

He shall remain,
And only He,
In brightest day,
In purest, radiant light.

(19th September 2014)

SAY NOT

Say not within your heart
He has forgotten,
He delays too long
In answering me.
Let not your heart be tempted
To be distressed
Or in disquietude.
He most surely hears and knows
Each one of your concerns –
Urgent or minute,
He carries each one with you.
He never loses interest
Nor puts off
His answer to your prayers.
His timing is most perfect –
You will not suffer needlessly.
He sees and knows all things.

But when He deems
The time is right
Then He shall move
On your behalf.
Your heart may rest
And quiet be,
So trust in Him
And banish
All anxiety.

(22nd September 2014)

HIS LIGHT

Within your heart
The light has come,
The dawn breaks forth
And scatters all the darkness.
You know His love.
And yet more is to come -
Until He shines
Like brightest noon,
The Sun of righteousness
With healing in His wings.

Fear not the things of old,
The wounds that hurt so deeply.
Trust in His love
And in His faithfulness.
His promise is He will give back
The years the locusts
Took away.
He shall fill all the deepest voids,
The chasms of emptiness.

So rest assured –
His love shall grow and shine
More deeply in your heart.
The day will come
When you can say in truth,
"He is my all in all."

(22nd October 2014)

FEAR NOT THE POISONED DART

Fear not the poisoned dart,
The arrow that aims to blame
And to fix guilt
Upon your heart.
It comes not from your Lord
But from a sullied source
That would let evil rule
And have its way.

The evil one knows well
The weakest link, your raw and tender spots
Of vulnerability.
His aim is sure.

But there stands a greater law
Which he most surely does not comprehend.
He will attempt to hurt and wound
And thinks he will succeed.

But you shall dwell in that
Secure and secret place
Of God Most High,
And there you shall abide;
His shadow will protect you.

And there beneath His wing
Shall be your refuge, and the place

To which you must turn and run.
God Most High shall be
Your dwelling place and sanctuary
And there no evil shall befall you.

Fear not the onslaught.
Look to Him, and then
All else will fall away
And gradually grow dim.

You then shall dwell in safety
And calm shall be your heart.
Fear not that great impostor
Or his evil darts.
He cannot touch you
When you abide in God.

(23rd November 2014)

DO NOT STRUGGLE SO

Do not struggle so
Against your present lot
Which comes from Me -
The drudgery,
Head bowed, nose to the grindstone.
Was it not the very same
Toil and weariness
That my Son knew?

The Son of God
Came down from Heaven itself,
And yet was subject
To earthly parents
And labour as a carpenter.
He did so for the joy
Set before Him,
Knowing too of the cross
That was to come.

Your time will also come
To be my messenger,
And my appointed one
For the task I have
Entrusted to your care.

Be patient then
And share your load with Him –

His yoke is easy
And His burden light.
So let your heart
Be filled with joy,
For I have chosen you
To follow in His steps.

(27th November 2014)

YOUR STRENGTH SHALL COME…

Your strength shall come
From waiting on your God,
And not from searching in your mind
Which way to go,
Which choice is best.

Much thought and calculation,
Debating back and forth
Will not help you find the path
That I have chosen for you.

My will for you
Is in unchartered waters,
Your path unique,
As for each one
Of my dear, precious children.

Before you were conceived
I knew you;
I formed you in the womb
According to my plans
And purposes.

But you must realise
Unless you dwell in Me
You will not know,
Will not discern
My will for you.

So wait on Me, your God,
Then you will know my peace,
And calm shall be your heart.
And when the time
Shall come,
Then you will know
With certainty of faith
What I will have you do.

So rush not here and there
And in your mind be calm
And wait upon your God.

(3rd December 2014)

I SEND THE SNOW

I send the snow,
I send the rain,
And they do not return
To Me.
They have a purpose to fulfil:
To irrigate the earth
And give it strength
To bring forth shoots and sprouts
That bud and flower
Then bear forth fruit and seed,
And so it is the sower once more
Can plant new seed,
And man can eat
His daily bread,
His sustenance.

So is it with my word.
I send it to your heart
In the same way,
To bring to life the seeds of faith
That I have planted there.
I plant, I water,
And the increase too, is mine,
So to my glory shall it be.

(9th December 2014)

STARS

I formed the heavens
And I made the stars,
I know their number.
I placed each one
Into its own unique orbit,
To shine
In the dark night
According to my purposes
And plans.
They shine for Me
And with the light I give.
They show forth my glory
And not their own.
According to my pleasure
I created them,
I saw that it was good.

And so it is with you.
I put my life, my light,
Into you, my earthen vessel,
That it should shine forth
And bring comfort, help and courage
To others along the way.
You shine not for your own delight
Or satisfaction;
Neither do you shine
For others to observe

Your earthen vessel
And say how marvellous it is
That such a simple vessel,
Made of clay,
Should shine so brilliantly.

But let your light so shine
That others may see
And glorify your Father
Who created you
For His own glory,
And who is
The light within you.

(15th December 2014)

THE YOUNGER SON

"I want what is mine,"
Said the younger son,
"I want to be free,
And do as I want,
Be myself, my own master,
My own man."

The father's heart was heavy and sad.
In vain had he urged
His younger son
To stay at home, find fulfilment there,
Take his place, find his part
In the wonderful heritage
Of his family home.
The father knew that all he could do
Was to let the younger son go
And find out for himself
What life was like
In an alien, hedonistic land.

With a light heart
The younger son departed
On his exhilarating, carefree journey,
As he thought.
With a spring in his step,
His fortune in a hidden pouch,
Ready to see the world for himself.

Life in the city was alluring, enticing;
Beyond his wildest dreams
Were the pleasures that money could buy.
He embraced them all
But also let slip
The values, the principles,
His father had taught him.
His life was an endless round
Of parties, wild nights
And friends without number.

When he first perceived
That his fortune was dwindling,
Slowly but surely
The so-called new "friends"
Abandoned him one by one,
Till one day he woke up
And realised,
His profligate living
Had resulted in this –
No friends, no roof nor bed,
Not even any food
To eat.

At that same time
The harvest failed,
And famine was rampant
In that alien land.
He begged for work
And found a wealthy man

Who sent him to feed the pigs
In his fields.

He happily would have eaten
The husks he gave the pigs –
The most unclean of animals.

He came to himself
And realised
How far he had fallen.
He thought of his father's house once more,
And longed to see his father.
But he knew too
Of his profound unworthiness.
Then it dawned upon him
That his father's servants
Had a far better life,
And plenty of food to eat.

Realising how low
He had fallen in sin,
He then knew the only way
To stay alive
Was to go back home
To his father.

Since the day he left home
His father had longed and ached
To see his son again.
Every day he would walk a long way
To see whether, perchance,

His son had decided
To come back home.

So when the son was walking home,
Yet still a long way off,
The father saw him
On the horizon.
"Could it just be my dear son,
Returning home again?"
The father's heart
Was filled with compassion
When he ascertained
It was indeed his son,
Painfully retracing his steps.
The father ran to meet him
And embraced him.
In vain did the son pronounce
That he was not fit to be his son,
But would willingly be his servant.

So happy and relieved,
With a rejoicing heart,
The father commanded his servants
To bring the best robe
For the son to wear,
A ring for his finger
And new sandals
For his bare and dusty feet,
Encrusted with dirt.
He gave orders
To prepare a big feast

And kill the fatted calf
So that all could celebrate
The return of his son.
He that was dead
Was now alive again.

Never again did the son
Want his 'freedom',
To do as he wished in life.
For now he understood
That his father knew best,
And to abide in his father's house
Was the wisest, safest way
To live.

(4th January 2015)

THE QUESTION I WOULD ASK

The question I would ask is this:
Do you really, truly know Him?
In the depths of your heart,
Right through to the very core
Of your being?
His Spirit
Dwelling in your heart,
Ruling every thought and act,
And feeling?

Have you experienced His axe
Cutting right through
To the very root
Of the old tree –
The old nature
That dwelt within you,
And taking it right out,
Replacing the old person
With His clean
And Holy Spirit?

Knowing about Him is good.
You see that He is kind,
You know that He cares and loves,
And it gives you hope,
Meaning and direction
Amidst this dark world
Of sin and pain,
Of violence and wrong.

But this alone is not enough
To make of you
A new creation,
A transformed person
Whose source and sustenance
Is God Himself,
With His unending love
Dwelling within your heart.

But to whatever point
You have attained
On your own unique
And personal journey,
I plead with you
Not to give up,
Or to be half-hearted,
But to keep on walking
In that one direction
That leads to Him;
And let Him move
Within your heart,
Doing the work
That He alone can do.
He will most surely
Make of you
A true child of God,
Filled with His love and life,
Glorifying Him.

(10th January 2015)

MY LIFE IN YOU

You try
So hard
To live up
To my standards.
You faithfully read my word
And pray,
And that is good.
You serve
Like Martha did of old;
You seek to reach the lost.
Great sacrifices too
You make –
Of time, career,
Job opportunities,
Financial gain,
Choosing not to
Live at ease
In a comfortable,
Unpolluted environment.

You give your time,
Your energies, your rest,
Your relaxation,
Your personal interests –
To try and further
My kingdom.

All this I know
And see,
And treasure.

Yet one thing
I would say to you:
What I would have you do
Is give up
Your hard, laborious efforts
That are so burdensome.

Abandon yourself
To Me,
And let Me live
My life in you.

(10th January 2015)

HIS PEACE

Amidst the noise
And turmoil,
The pressures and demands
That clamour constantly,
And try
To take away your calm;
There is a quiet place
Of peace, tranquillity,
Where God reigns,
Right in the eye of the storm.

It can be found
When your heart is stilled,
Holding itself
Before Him.
You may be kneeling
In your quiet place,
Or being jostled
In the hustle and bustle
Of life's events
Which you cannot avoid,
Yet your heart is still,
Worshipping God,
Knowing the peace
That He alone can give -
A peace that the world
Knows nothing of,

A peace known only to those
Who fellowship constantly
In their hearts
With Him.
Be they mothers with clamouring children,
Or employees under the strain
Of unreasonable demands and stress;
Be they those with heavy burdens
Of responsibility for others,
Saddened by the sorrow of seeing
Broken hearts and broken lives,
Or ordinary folk in a wicked world
Endeavouring to lead a godly life;
Be they those with unbearable, crushing loads
Of grief and loss and distress,
Or martyrs facing imminent death;
Be they those whose bodies
Are racked with pain,
Sickness and suffering,
Or those enduring years
Of endless, boring daily routine;
Be they victims of injustice, violence, hate,
Or those who try to reconcile
The irreconcilable.

The circumstances matter not,
His promise stands:
"Peace I leave with you,
My peace I give to you;
Not as the world gives
Give I to you."

So let not your heart be troubled,
Nor let it be afraid,
In doubt or in distress.
In God there is a place of peace,
A peace the world cannot know.
A peace that cannot
Be taken away.

(11th January 2015)

LIFE ETERNAL

Life eternal
Springs from
A heavenly source.
It cannot be quenched
Or stifled,
And men cannot
Suppress or suffocate it.
It will only return
More strongly, more forcefully
Than before.
Just like a blade of grass
Will burst through
A small crack
In the concrete:
Pull it out
But it will only
Grow again,
For you cannot destroy
Its root
Or the seed
From which it came.

Two thousand years ago
Men tried to do
This very thing.
"Away with Him," they shouted,
Sending Him to the cross,

Thinking that this would bring an end
To the unease
In their consciences,
And that they could stamp out
The voice of God.

Jesus went to the cross,
But death could not hold
That pure and sinless life.
He rose again,
And instead of putting an end
To His voice, to His life,
His death and resurrection
Brought new birth,
Eternal life,
Into the hearts of men, women, children –
Untold numbers
Across the globe,
Down through the ages,
Just as He said:
"I have come
That you may have life."
The word of God,
His life,
Shall stand
Eternally.

(13th January 2015)

THE TRUTH

Many voices,
Insistent, conflicting voices,
All claiming to be
The truth.
They have their arguments,
Carefully constructed,
Intellectually watertight –
Or so they seem
At first to be.
They confuse,
Enslave the gullible
And bind them
With rules and regulations,
Precepts and courses of action
To follow,
By which one can be saved –
So they say.
This I have seen
So many times,
The outcome the very opposite
To what Jesus said.

He said, with God's authority,
"I am the way, the truth, and the life.
No man comes to the Father
But by Me."
His life, His death,

His resurrection
The proof of what He said.
He saved the lost, healed the sick,
Raised the dead,
Changed sinners' hearts,
And taught men how to live.
He loved us with the love of God,
Going to the cross
So that we could have
Eternal life.
He said each man
Should know God for himself.
His words were and are
Spirit and life.
He came, not to condemn
But that men might be saved
Through Him.

So beware of those
Who would put heavy burdens
Around the necks
Of others.
Burdens so weighty
To bear,
And which do not bring life,
But only rules, regulations
And obligations
To earn one's salvation
By doing this and that,
Memorizing books and passages
And doctrines of men.

But Jesus said
To those who believed in Him
And who continued in His word,
"You shall know the truth
And the truth
Will set you free."

                                                                                          (14th January 2015)

HIS WAYS

He has a habit
Of turning the way
Things are
In this world
Upside down.
The weak are made strong,
The mourners comforted,
The meek inheriting the earth,
The poor made rich in Him;
The merciful
Obtain mercy,
The humble are exalted,
The persecuted
Rejoice in God,
And the lame take the prey.

So beware
Of this world's standards.
They are most surely
Not the way of life
That God ordained
For us.
Neither are they
The way God thinks.
And He alone
Can be
Our standard and our measure
In this lost world
Of sin and pain.   (14th January 2015)

SIN

Sin –
That ugly, deformed,
Vile, repulsive root
That like a virulent plague,
Mars, cripples, disfigures,
Kills and destroys.

But what could be wrong
With tasting a forbidden fruit,
Seemingly so insignificant?
Or taking that small step
That my conscience tells me
Is not right?
Or a small toddler
Who seems so innocent,
Yet stubbornly defies his parents?
Surely it will not affect the outcome
In the great scheme of things?
But it does.

The root of such philosophy
Comes not from God.
If allowed to run its course
The final outcome can result
In untold grief and misery:
Murder, hatred, genocide,
Violence, torture and brutality,

Unending tragedies,
Unimaginable pain and loss
And grief of heart,
Inflicting wounds that can never heal
Unless God Himself intervenes.

But He has –
Dying in ignominy
On that cruel cross,
Suffering the most brutal death
That wicked man could invent,
Yet suffering even more
Of a broken heart,
And agony that produced
Sweat drops of blood –
Because of my sin
And incredulity,
So that I could be forgiven
And that His Spirit
Could come and live
Within my heart.

Thanks be to God
For His incomparable,
Utterly indescribable
Gift of love!

(21st January 2015)

LORD AND KING

When the Son of God
Came into the world,
Without any pomp or fanfare
Or welcoming ceremony,
Just a message to ordinary shepherds
Watching their sheep –
An angel appeared and announced
The birth of a Saviour,
Not a king.
This was great news
For all mankind
And the heavenly host
Praised God
And sang this amazing message
Of peace on earth
And God's goodwill
To mankind.

A humble stable
Was His first abode;
Then followed escape
To an alien land
With His earthly parents –
A refugee family
Fleeing for safety;
Then returning again
When God's messenger

Informed them
That it was safe
To do so.

As Jesus grew
He was constantly in communion
With His Father in heaven.
We know not what He went through
During those thirty years of waiting,
But there must have been much
To grieve His heart.

Then finally the time came
For His public ministry.
Seeing His miracles
Many believed in His name,
But Jesus did not commit Himself
To them,
Because He knew what was in man,
And He had come
As a Saviour
To deliver from sin.

When He fed the five thousand
The crowds marvelled.
They wanted to take Him by force
And make Him King,
But it was a human king they wanted –
To have a better life,
To be free from Roman occupation,
To have someone who stood higher than others,

Who could perform miracles
And who could change things.

They never thought about
What God had in mind
Because they were not seeking
His will.
So Jesus quickly departed
By Himself
To the mountain
To be alone with God.

The scribes and the Pharisees –
The religious men of the day –
Were increasingly incensed
As time went on.
Who did this apparently untrained,
Uneducated man
Think he was?
But there was a much more fundamental reason
For their anger.
The more they heard
Of what Jesus said and did,
And the fragrance of His life,
The more deeply it disturbed
Their consciences
And threatened their authority
And power
With the people.
They bode their time,
But did not realise

That they were conforming
To God's own timetable.

Eventually the point came
When Jesus knew
That His disciples finally realised
That He had come from God.

It was Jesus Himself,
In unity of purpose with His Father,
Who set things in motion
And allowed Judas
To carry out his nefarious purpose
And betray Him
For financial gain.

After His arrest
The fickle crowd
Turned against Him.
They asserted that Jesus
Was not the king they wanted –
They knew no other king than Caesar.

Pilate was amazed
That Jesus said nothing
In defence of Himself.
He asked Him whether He was not
A king.
Jesus simply and calmly replied
That His kingdom was not of this world.
If it were, His servants would fight

On His behalf
And not allow
This turn of events.

So Jesus went to the cross.
He knew all along
That this was what He must do
To save mankind.
But death could not hold
That pure and sinless life.
He rose again,
Appeared to His disciples,
And after forty days
Ascended to heaven,
Where now He sits
On the throne
At His Father's right hand,
As King of kings
And Lord of lords.

But the question now remains
For each and every one of us
To answer
In the depths of our own hearts:
Will we agree to let this King,
Who also is our Saviour,
Reign in our hearts and lives?

(31st January 2015)

WORSHIP

There is a place in God
Where my heart prostrates itself
In silence
And simply worships Him.
It is a place beyond words,
Beyond needs, desires
Or prayer requests,
Beyond clamour or problems,
Even songs of praise,
A place of pure abandonment
To Him
Where being in His presence
Stills and hushes all else,
And He is all in all.

Times there are
When all I can do
Is bow my head
In silence -
My heart overwhelmed
With His grace and love
And what He does
On my behalf.
Then my heart
Simply prostrates itself
And worships Him.

(3rd February 2015)

JEW AND GENTILE

In the beginning
It was not so.
God created man
According to His own image.
There was no thought
Of nations or peoples,
Classes or divisions.
But then the greatest tragedy of all
Occurred.
Man chose to disobey God.
This was a betrayal
Of such magnitude
That we can only understand
In some minute measure
How deeply we had rejected
And offended God.

But God's heart is one of love
And though He could and should have
Condemned us all to death,
He chose instead
To suffer
On our behalf.

He put His plan of redemption
Into effect.
But the grief and pain it caused

To the Godhead
Is hard for us
To even begin to imagine.
To see Cain
Slaying his own brother –
And this kind of evil
Action and intent
Repeated
Over and over again.

God later had to flood the earth
Because of our great sin:
He had somehow to make us understand
That good and evil,
Light and darkness
Can never co-exist.
He regretted creating mankind.
But Noah – the only man on the earth
At that time
Who feared and respected God,
Found grace in God's eyes,
And so was saved.

When Noah came out of the ark
He built an altar to the Lord
And offered sacrifices
Of every clean animal and bird.
God smelt the aroma and vowed
That never again
Would He flood the earth.
Thus God's plan of redemption

Was never forgotten
Or annulled.

Then later unrepentant man
Wanted to reach heaven
And built a high tower.
God then had no option
But to destroy the tower
And scatter man
All over the earth.
He confounded our languages
So that we could not do the same thing again.
None of this was easy
For God to do.
He had all the power,
But His heart of love
Was grieved, hurt and broken,
Over and over again.

He never forgot for a moment
His redemption plan.
And in His heart
This plan of salvation
Was for all mankind.

But in order for us
To understand God,
His heart, His ways,
And for a chosen few
To be able to finally recognise
The Saviour when He came,

God had to choose
A special people
As His very own –
To teach them His ways
And His character,
His laws,
And what He planned to do.
So He sent many messengers
To show the way,
To teach Israel
How to live.

But they were often stiff-necked,
Disobedient,
And continued to cause
Grief of heart
And despair.

God never gave up
Because He knew
The power of His own life,
And that the sacrifice
Of His most precious Son
Would make it possible
For God and man
To dwell in unity.

When Jesus came to the earth,
He was born in Bethlehem.
The wise men came
From a far country

To visit Him at His birth.
And the message of the angels
To local shepherds
Was that a Saviour had been born
For all mankind.

But He had to come
First to the Jews
Or no-one would ever know
Where He was from
Or what He had come to do.

Those who willingly heard Him
Sometimes thought He was
The promised Messiah,
But had their own ideas
As to what this meant.

Jesus, however, clearly said,
Speaking of the cross to come,
That when He was lifted up
He would draw all men
To Himself.
He was in no way exclusive –
But the Saviour of the world.

Even after His death and resurrection
The apostles and disciples
Were slow to understand this truth.

God had to use extraordinary measures
To help them understand –
Involving angels, visions, delegations
And direct outpourings
Of His Holy Spirit.

But finally
They that truly knew Him
In their hearts,
Understood the universal nature
Of His love.

He has broken down
The middle wall
That separated Jew and Gentile,
And any other division
That man has set up.
Of the two He made one –
One people, one church,
His people
Who live
To worship Him.

(5th February 2015)

MY SHEEP HEAR MY VOICE

Fret not yourself
About the future –
Whether you will make the grade,
Succeed or not succeed,
In the next stage of your life.
Worry not
About the passage of time,
Getting older
And not having achieved
Very much.
Is He not your Good Shepherd
Who leads you
Each step of the way?

Worry not
About not recognising
His voice
And choosing the wrong path.
Has He not promised
To be your guide?
He said nothing
About sheep needing to be clever,
Or obtaining such and such a grade
In order to recognise
The way.

There is no special course
Or guidance book
For them to read.
Life in God
Is much simpler
Than what we often think.

He said very clearly,
And still does today,
That His sheep do hear and know
His voice.
He goes before them,
And they follow.
They will not follow
A stranger
Because they are clearly aware
That it is
An unfamiliar voice.

Jesus is the One
Who does the speaking,
And the leading,
And all we need to do
Is follow Him.

Has it not come to your attention
That the sheep we see every day
In the fields,
On the hills,
Are not worried
About getting it wrong?

So why cannot we
Take Him at His word?

(17th February 2015)

BE STILL

Be still, my soul, and know
That He is God
And He alone.
No room for that small
Yet pernicious word, 'but',
Which, like an addiction,
Creeps its way into
All sorts of situations,
And destroys
Or weakens
The seed of faith.
Listen not to that voice,
Which also raises
Many doubts and protestations:
'What if', 'if only', 'it's too late',
Or 'no one understands'.

His word is incisive and alive,
Keen and penetrating,
Sharper than any
Two-edged sword.
It will never fail
To hit the mark.
Then let it do its work.
Do not dispute
Or strive against it.
Its purpose is to expunge

And then to heal.

The wisest choice
Is to bow down
And recognise His Lordship.
Therefore be still, my soul,
And know that He,
And He alone
Is God.

(18th February 2015)

WEAKNESS

Despise not
Your own weakness
For in it
Lies your strength.

Was it not in utter weakness
That our Saviour
Came into this world,
Born as a helpless, defenceless babe,
Entrusted to the care
Of the most ordinary of mortals,
In a country under foreign occupation
Where a ruthless puppet king
Destroyed any hint of threat
Or challenge
To his rule
By slaughtering
Both babes and infants?

How could God the Father
Allow His most precious Son
To encounter such danger
When in His most defenceless state?

But God the Father
Knows and trusts
The power of His own life and Spirit.

Why then should we fear
Any state of weakness
In our own lives?

God Himself has declared
It is in our weakness
That His strength is made perfect.
His grace
Is sufficient
To carry us through.
But, human as we are,
We often like to have reserves
Of strength, of power, of ability,
As some kind of backup plan
To help us through.
But that is not His way.

We should then rejoice
In our inabilities
So that God's power and strength
May manifest themselves
In a world
Which has things back to front
And upside down.
The strong tread down the weak,
The proud mock the meek and humble,
The infirm are pushed aside,
Money and power
Hold sway.
But that is not how it is
In His kingdom.

There the lame take the prey
And the meek inherit the earth.

Therefore rejoice
In weakness and infirmity,
Of being in waters
That are far too deep
For us to get through
On our own.
Thus shall His name,
And not that of a mortal man,
Be glorified.

(20th February 2015)

WHAT I WOULD SAY

Remember this:
That God has planted
His most precious seed
Within your heart.
The treasure He has given you
Is of far greater worth
Than anything
This world or any man
Can offer you.
Of much greater value than all the silver,
Gold and precious gems and pearls
This world has ever held.
Worth more than power,
Fame or wealth,
Countries and lands,
And all the vast resources
They contain.
More precious even
Than the closest, dearest
Human ties of love
That man can know.

It is His pure and spotless life
That He has put
Within your heart.

Eternal life is to know Him,
The one and only God eternal,
Revealed to us
Through His Son, Jesus Christ.

So bury not this treasure
In some forgotten place
Deep within.
You must commune with Him
And worship at His feet,
Your heart in adoration,
Full of wonder,
At this great work of glory,
Salvation and redemption –
That God should choose to dwell
In you
And me.
So allow not your life
To be dictated to
By the pressures of this world,
Your job, and all that
It demands,
Your family, friends,
Society.

God has planted His seed
Within your heart.
He will water and nourish it,
But we must give Him space and time,
And consciously allow Him
To do so.

Forget not this most precious thing.
It is of greater worth
Than all the world.

(24th February 2015)

PRIDE

God says in His Word,
'By pride comes nothing but strife',
And He is the One who knows
And understands
Far better than any other.

Pride brings hardness of heart,
Unwillingness to bend the knee,
And to accept another.
It brings destruction
On an unimaginable scale;
It wounds and hurts,
And causes scars so deep
That only God Himself can heal.
It causes me to weep,
And yet I only know and see
Such a minute part
Of its destructive force.
It separates, causes division,
And brings about wars,
Dissension and strife.

It is an ugly monster
That dares to look at God
In a wilful, mocking way,
Refusing to accept
His authority.

It repudiates all humility
And therefore rejects
God's very heart.

Be it personal, regional, ethnic or national,
Or loyalty to a clan or group or clique,
It is all the same
In its root cause.
Does it not come from the same source
As Lucifer of old,
Who in his heart aspired
To exalt his throne
Above the stars of God
And be like the Most High?

But God could not allow him
To take the throne –
All that is good and pure and holy
Would then be lost forever.
And we can only overcome him,
That evil one,
In our own personal lives,
By the blood of the Lamb,
And the word of our testimony.

So yield not to pride of heart –
It causes nothing but strife
On an unimaginable scale.

(26th February 2015)

HARDSHIP

To endure hardship
Is part of my walk with Him.
A good soldier I desire to be,
Pleasing to my great commander,
And I would honour Him.

So therefore it is
That I have need
To be so clear
In my priorities –
The way I spend my time.
Life is so short –
I cannot allow myself
To be pulled in all directions.
God is my first pursuit,
My only true pursuit,
And all else
Must fall in line.

He knows when I need
To be refreshed
Or to rest a while.
And He does not overdrive
Or overburden
His sheep.

But I must listen constantly

To His voice,
And obey
Immediately.
Would not a soldier
In any regular army
Be alert to all commands
From those above him?
I then should be
Even more alert
To the voice of Him
Who is Lord of all,
And King of kings.
All my interests, desires, ambitions,
Goals and inclinations
Must and shall
Be governed by Him.
I must not be diverted
By distractions
Or go down some sidetrack
That would channel some of my energies
Away from Him.

Then, when I meet Him
Face to face
I shall have no regrets
And will not be ashamed.
Hardship therefore
I most willingly will suffer,
For it is for His sake.
As the Master,
So shall the servant be. (6th March 2015)

BEING MISUNDERSTOOD

It is painful
To be misunderstood
By others.
Sometimes I think
There is hardly a soul
Who really understands
What I am going through,
What I have to bear
Alone,
And what my heart really is.

Comments and actions,
Or lack of action or understanding,
Cut deep
And add to the pain.

And yet I must not
Feel sorry for myself.
Jesus Himself walked this path
With only the Father in Heaven
Understanding
What He was going through –
Bearing the sin of us all.

And as for me,
The Father knows and understands
The pain of heart and body,

The struggles in my soul.
He knows my ways,
He knows my attitude of heart,
And understands my intentions,
My desires.
Is that not enough?

It is!
And so I will continue
To commune with Him,
Sometimes in tears,
Sometimes in joy.
But I commit all things
To Him
Who knows me.

(7th March 2015)

WHERE JOY IS FOUND

Outside of God
Pure, unmitigated joy
Does not exist –
That joy inexpressible
And full of glory –
The world knows it not.
Even man's sublimest moments
Outside of Him
Are marred
By sin or pride,
Or some regret,
Or simply by an emptiness
Caused by the absence of His presence –
He by whom and for whom
All things were made.

Seek not for joy or true delight
Outside of Him.
It can only be a transient,
Fleeting thing
That fades away and disappears
Like morning dew,
As quickly as a puff of wind.

In His presence
And in His presence alone,
Is fullness of joy.

But oh the joy
Of knowing Him
Dwelling deep
Within my heart!

(8th March 2015)

SERVING HIM

First I must know Him
Deep within,
Then let Him rule
My heart and life.
In all things it is He
Who must hold sway;
I need to yield
And to allow Him
To govern in my life –
Not begrudgingly
But because I love Him,
He who first loved me.

So I present my body
A living sacrifice,
Holy and acceptable to Him,
Because He dwells in me.
I must not conform myself
To this world and its ways.
How can I,
When He is the treasure
Within my heart,
In this plain earthen vessel?

I must think soberly
And not hold
Too high an estimation

Of myself
Or my spirituality.
He will teach me how to think
In a right and proper way,
Acceptable to Him,
According to the measure of faith
That He has granted me.
We all have different functions
In this life,
But He alone decides
What He created
Each to be.

He is the treasure
In this earthen vessel
Made of the most commonplace
Of clay.
So I become the bearer
Of this pearl of greatest price.
Others sometimes will marvel
And I must let them see
And understand
The preciousness is not the clay
But He who dwells within.
And I would not detract
One single jot
From His great worth.

I am here on this earth
But for a season,
Then He will take me

To be with Him.
My privilege then
Is to point the way
To Him who gave Himself
For us all,
And let others see
That to know Him
Is life eternal.

(9th March 2015)

JUDGING OTHERS

We who go around
With planks in our eyes,
Have we nothing better to do
Than in our semi-blindness
To look for tiny specks
In the eyes of others?
Our minds and understanding
Are so dim,
There is so much
We cannot comprehend
Or grasp,
Yet in passing judgment
On others
We are both expert and hasty.

Are we not foolish?
Even dangerously so?
Judgment brings division,
Cuts people off
From each other.
It separates,
Engenders pride,
Feelings of superiority –
The very opposite
Of the love of God
And the tender heart
Of our Saviour.

He did not come among us
To crush and to destroy,
But to save,
And to restore.

God Himself has told us
Time and time again
To leave all judgment to Him,
For He alone sees and knows
Things as they truly are.
And who are we to judge
When God says
He has the ability
To make our brother, sister
Stand before Him?
And with whatever measure we employ to judge
We shall be judged ourselves.

(16th March 2015)

THERE IS A LIFE. . .

There is a life
Within my heart
That would rise up,
A voice
That would speak out
Of God's great love,
Of His great might,
Of His supreme and boundless
Worthiness.
My heart so longs
To urge the world
To listen
To the voice of God,
To worship Him.

Yet I am nothing –
This I know full well,
Merely a simple vessel
Made by Him
And for His use.
But choose I must
To follow Him
And go wherever He leads.

So I will stir myself,
And let the life
He put within

Rise up and honour Him.
It may not be that I have
Mighty words to speak,
But I can let His Spirit flow
And have free reign in me.
The vessel matters not.

But this I know
That God's own Holy Spirit
Both moves and flows
According to His will,
And He will do great things
If only I will let Him move.

It matters not
That no one sees or knows
What God is telling me to do.
Obey I will
And leave the rest to Him.
So shall His name be glorified
And sanctified
Within my heart.

(19th March 2015)

Eleri Wynne

NEW LIFE

Spring has come.
Leaves of the freshest green
Appear on trees and bushes,
Blossom breaks out,
Encouraged by the sun's warm glow,
And birds return from hotter climes
With their rejoicing songs.
Nature declares –
It is the season of new life.

What God would have us understand
Is mirrored all around –
That life proceeds from death.
The seed the farmer plants
To all intents is dead
Unless he waters it
And the warmth of the bright spring sun
Compels it to break through
The outer husk
And then push forth new shoots.
Jesus said,
In order for a corn of wheat
To yield a crop of grain
It must first fall into the ground
And die.
But if it dies,
It will most surely bear forth fruit,

For God will water it
And give it all the warmth it needs.

Jesus was speaking
Of spiritual things,
But we whose minds are dim
Need parables to understand,
Parables that emanate from God.

The greatest truth
That God would have us comprehend
Is this:
That Jesus died for us,
Was crucified
Upon that cruel cross,
Then buried in a tomb
Hewn out in a rock
And sealed with a huge stone.
But Jesus conquered death –
His sinless life could not be held
By the results of sin.
He rose again,
Ascended back to heaven,
So that we, unworthy ones,
Down through the ages,
Across the globe,
Could live
Through the matchless sacrifice
He made for us.

So spring reminds us
Of this eternal truth,
And would reveal yet more
To our dull minds.
If we be willing
To lay down our lives
And let God have His way,
New life shall come
And we will bear much fruit
Through Him, for Him,
And glorify His name.

(21st March 2015)

THE SUFFERINGS OF CHRIST

Long have I pondered
What God really meant by
"Making up what is lacking
In the afflictions of Christ."
For I know full well
That His Son's death and sacrifice
Is sufficient
For every human being
That ever lived, lives now
Or yet to be born -
For us all to know God
And be born again
Of His Spirit.
There can be nothing lacking
In that sacrifice
That procured our salvation,
It says so in God's word.
And yet those words are there,
Also given by God.

Then it began to dawn within my heart
And slowly then I realised
That what God meant
Was that the life of Christ
In me could suffer,
So that at times
My heart is deeply grieved

By what I see and hear and know,
And things I have to go through –
Grieved and tried to a degree
That is hard to endure.

It has nothing to do with what I am,
Or have achieved or not achieved;
It is rather the Spirit of Jesus
Suffering within my heart,
And in the heart of my brother
Or sister.

So let us be encouraged
And worship Him,
Giving thanks
That we are counted worthy
To take part in His sufferings.

(25th March 2015)

THERE IS A HOLY FIRE

There is a holy fire
That comes from God
That wants to burn
And burn continually
In each believer's heart.
It is the life of God.

This fire will not come down
Unless we welcome Him in,
Unless our longing is
That all else be consumed
And that we live
To honour Him
And Him alone.

Fire burns all the dross,
All that comes not from God,
All that is transient and fleeting,
All that is not pure gold.

I desire not
What the world says
It can give me:
Financial security,
A reliable job,
Pleasures, delights,
Connections, introductions,

Entertainment,
Ways to achieve my goals,
Plans and purposes,
And all that money can buy.

These pleasures are not what they seem –
At first attractive,
But in the long run
They contain deep emptiness,
For it is the evil one
Trying to entice us
Away from God.
But my desire is to honour God
And do that which withstands the fire.
If He entrusts me with work to do,
Puts purposes in my heart,
Then He himself supplies the means,
And I need not resort
To the "sensible" ways of man.

I am not hotheaded and crazy,
Without forethought or common sense,
I have seriously counted the cost
And my heart's decision is to honour Him.

So I lay myself on His altar,
My life I yield to Him.
I will not take it back again.
He can do as He sees fit –
My privilege is to honour Him.

(30th March 2015)

THANKSGIVING

I have so much
To be thankful for.
He sought me when I was
In great anguish of heart,
Saved me from sin and death,
Came into my heart to live
And gave me deep joy and peace,
Such as I had never known before.

He has taught me,
Step by step,
To walk with Him,
Guided me safely through countless trials,
Shown me what life is all about,
And has never let me down.

He has kept me,
Been patient with me,
Comforted me when I needed comfort,
Corrected me when I was wrong,
Healed my anguish of heart,
Saved me from innumerable dangers –
Some I am aware of,
Others I know nothing about.

He has taken me deeper
Into Himself, His life.

He has loved me like none other,
With an everlasting love,
And has promised and convinced me
That He will never let me go.

He has established
His calling on my life,
And given me the honour
Of serving Him.

None of this have I ever deserved –
This I know through and through.
But He has called me to be
His very own,
And deeply imprinted His will
Upon my heart.
He has given me purpose in my life –
A purpose worth living
And dying for.

How can I not be thankful
In the face of such stupendous grace?
My heart is eternally grateful
To Him, my Saviour,
My Lord and my God.

(30th March 2015)

HOLY GROUND

There are times in life
When we are suddenly aware
That we are standing on holy ground –
Where we hardly dare
To place a foot,
Or even dare to move or breathe.

Sometimes it is our hallowed God
Touching our lives
In a special way.
Other times it is His holy presence
In the life of another,
Or a very distinct awareness
That our most holy God Himself
Is at work,
In such a way
That we can only
Bow our heads in reverence
And listen to Him.

We must never forget
That He who is our closest friend
And comforter,
Is at the same time
The most Holy God
From on High.

(4th April 2015)

YOU HAVE A WAY

You have a way
Of creating a path in the wilderness,
Where nothing but sand
Or barren ground
Can be seen,
And human hope has failed;
Where it is impossible
For the human mind or eye
To find a way
That leads to water
And to life.
But you speak,
And gently lead us
To the place of living waters
That abounds with life.

You have a way
Of leading us
Through such thick darkness
That is almost palpable,
And nothing can be seen.
You speak your word
Into our hearts
And we follow your leading,
Until you bring us through
To light and bright sunshine
Once more.

You have a way
Of comforting those
In deepest distress
And almost devoid of hope.
You gently draw near
And cause us
To see Yourself once more
Through our tears and pain,
Causing us to know
We are not alone.
For you are the God
Who comforts the comfortless.

You have a way….
When strength has failed,
Our bodies weak, our health worn down,
You reveal your love
And infinite care for us.
You carry us through
Where our own strength
Has reached its utmost limits.
You open our eyes to see
That the life of God
Depends not on bodily strength
But on your power alone.

In every circumstance
You yourself are the way,
And we can forever abide
Under the shadow
Of the Almighty God. (4th April 2015)

KNOWING HIM

Knowing Him
Is life eternal.

Knowing His love,
Deep within our hearts -
A love that human beings
And even angels
Cannot comprehend.

Knowing His grace,
Sufficient for each day's needs –
One day at a time.

Knowing His forgiveness
That pardons all our sin,
And gives us the ability
To pardon those who hurt us.

Knowing His truth
Which sets us free
In every circumstance.

Knowing His peace –
Greater than any storm,
Worry or calamity,
And keeps our hearts
Fixed on Him.

Knowing His word –
A lamp for our feet,
Giving us direction,
Showing us which way to go.

Knowing His comfort
In all our troubles
And anxieties,
Through His Spirit
Who dwells within.

Knowing His faith –
A gift from Him,
Enabling us to trust Him.

Knowing His hope
When humanly all is lost,
So we need not despair.
Knowing His ways
Which He reveals
To those who love Him
And look to Him.

Knowing Him –
Jesus the hope of glory
Living within our hearts:
This is life eternal.

(21st May 2015)

PASSING JUDGMENT

Who can discern the thoughts of a man?
God and His Spirit alone.
Who can pierce through the intents of our hearts?
God and His Spirit alone.
Who then can judge a fellow man,
Can know what his motives are?
Unless God reveals His own thoughts to us,
It is better for us not to rashly pronounce
But rather wait patiently
For God to speak.

For His ways are not our ways,
His thoughts much higher than ours,
As the heavens are higher than the earth.
The Lord will have mercy
And pardon abundantly
Where we mere mortals,
Though clearly aware of His goodness and grace
In our lives,
Will write off or classify
As a loser
A dear, precious soul
Who has not quite made it yet.

We cannot and must not judge
The servant of another,
For it is his own master who decides

Whether he stands or falls,
And God is well able
To make him stand.
And He alone knows
Who will stand before Him
Upon that final day.

(18th June 2015)

THAT WHICH COMES OUT OF THE HEART

Sometimes it seems to me
That Christians forget,
Or have never really grasped,
What Jesus meant when He said
That it is not
What goes into the mouth
That defiles a man or a woman,
But rather
That which comes out of the mouth:
For those are the things
Which come out of our hearts –
And they are the origin
Of all kinds of sin and evil thoughts:
Murder, adultery, thieving, lies,
Betrayals and blasphemies.
So rather than try so hard
To keep young people
And even adults
From beer and wine,
Gourmet dining, smoking, karaoke bars,
Worldly music, make-up, jewellery,
Fashionable or designer clothes and shoes,
'Doubtful' places, people and activities,
And associating with anyone
Who practises, encourages or is not against
These things,
Should we not be concentrating rather

On the heart of the gospel?
And not regarding the people who we think
Are touching or embracing worldly things
As having a deadly pestilence,
Telling others to keep a very safe distance
From them,
Lest we ourselves become infected?

Jesus came to make of us a new creation,
With God's own Spirit living in our hearts
And showing us the way,
Guiding our every step.
He said,
"When I am lifted up
I will draw all men to me."

That drawing is irresistible
To a hungry heart,
And hearts are not made hungry
By lists of dos and don'ts,
But by the very life of God,
Come in the flesh.

(23rd June 2015)

HIS SUPPLY

God never runs out
Of resources,
His supplies
Will never dry up.
He is an abundant God –
The maker and owner
Of the universe,
Yet abounding, overflowing,
In kindness, mercy and grace,
With love unfailing
And without end.

It is we who limit Him
Because of our lack of trust and faith,
Not knowing Him well enough.
We limit the number of vessels we bring
To be filled with His oil,
Like the widow of old.
We seek for signs and put out fleeces,
Not once, but repeatedly,
As Gideon did,
In order to have proof
That God means what He says,
And that we have not misunderstood.
We hesitate,
Hardly daring
To ask for more,

Or let God enlarge our hearts.

He who comes to God
Must not only believe that God is
Who He says He is,
But that He also rewards
Those who earnestly seek Him.

The river of life
Which comes from God
Will never run dry.
It cannot do so.
His treasury, like He Himself,
Is eternally abundant,
Ever new.
But unless we draw near
In faith,
Believe, and receive from Him,
Despite God's unending bounty,
We may never know
The richness of His life and love.

(17th July 2015)

THE KINGDOM OF GOD

Jesus said
That the kingdom of God
Is like the seed
Of a mustard tree.
When it is planted
It is very small,
But God waters it
And it grows,
Almost imperceptibly
At first.
But slowly and surely
It gets broader and taller,
Developing in strength
As it grows.
God continues to shower it
With all that it needs,
Of rain and sun,
So that in the end
The birds of the air
Can nest and find shelter
In its branches.

He also said
That the kingdom of God
Is like yeast
Which a baker puts
Into a bowl of flour

And waits
Until the dough
Has risen.
By the end
There will be no part
Of the dough
Unaffected
By the yeast.

And so
Does His kingdom grow
In an individual heart.
The seed is well and truly planted,
Then God ordains the rain
And causes the circumstances
That produce the increase,
Till all in that life
Gives glory to God.

His church too,
Grows in this fashion.
The three thousand souls
Added on the Day of Pentecost
Were only possible
Because of the three and a half years
That Jesus patiently spent
With His disciples,
Planting the seed,
Watering it,
Until the disciples realised
Who He was in truth.

He died on the cross
And rose again,
So His Spirit could be poured
Into their hearts –
God the Father
Giving the increase.

So let us be patient
And not despise
The day of small things.

(18th July 2015)

I KNOW NOT HOW

I know not how
I have come through
These years:
The circumstances
That overwhelmed me,
Waters too deep,
Too treacherous
To steer my way through
On my own;
Sickness, weakness,
Suffering,
Weariness and pain
That in my own strength
I could never have endured.
Loneliness and isolation,
The incomprehension
And misunderstanding
Of others;
The loss of dear friends,
Hardships I baulked at,
Yet had to go undergo;
Responsibilities
That weighed heavily
Upon me;
Situations
That troubled me,
And difficulties

That were impossible to solve.

Yet through all these things
He kept me and held me,
Spoke to my heart
And sustained me,
Provided for my every need,
And comforted my soul.
It is by His grace
And His provision alone
That I stand.

There is nothing
That I regret.
He ordained my path
And knew what I needed
To become strong in Him
And secure in His love.
So today I stand
With a thankful heart,
Confident in Him.

It is He
Who has carried me
Through these years,
And I am privileged
To be counted
His child.

(19th July 2015)

Printed in Great Britain
by Amazon